TERRORIST ATTACKS

THE ATTACKS ON THE WORLD TRADE CENTER

FEBRUARY 26, 1993, AND SEPTEMBER 11, 2001

Carolyn Gard

The Rosen Publishing Group, Inc.
New York

To all who lost their lives in the attacks
on the World Trade Center

Published in 2003 by The Rosen Publishing Group, Inc.
29 East 21st Street, New York, NY 10010

First Edition

Library of Congress Cataloging-in-Publication Data

Gard, Carolyn.
The attacks on the World Trade Center: February 26, 1993, and
September 11, 2001 / by Carolyn Gard. — 1st ed.
    p. cm. — (Terrorist attacks)
Summary: A comprehensive look at the World Trade Center towers, the 1993
bombing and the attacks of September 11, 2001 that brought them down, the
terrorists involved, and America's response.
Includes bibliographical references and index.
ISBN 0-8239-3657-0 (lib. bdg.: alk. paper)
1. Terrorism—United States. 2. World Trade Center Bombing, New York, N.Y.,
1993. 3. September 11 Terrorist Attacks, 2001. 4. Bin Laden, Osama, 1957–
[1. Terrorism. 2. World Trade Center Bombing, New York, N.Y., 1993.
3. September 11 Terrorist Attacks, 2001. 4. Bin Laden, Osama, 1957–]
I. Title. II. Series.
HV6432 .G37 2003
974.7'1043—dc21
2002001034
                                                                    2001007029

Manufactured in the United States of America

CONTENTS

	Introduction	5
Chapter 1	The World Trade Center Towers	9
Chapter 2	September 11, 2001	19
Chapter 3	The Official Response	31
Chapter 4	Osama bin Laden	41
Chapter 5	Fighting Terrorism	49
Chapter 6	The Reaction	55
	Glossary	59
	For More Information	60
	For Further Reading	61
	Bibliography	62
	Index	63

This aerial view shows the area on which stood the two 110-story twin towers of New York City's World Trade Center. Only a portion of the devastation caused by the terror attacks of September 11, 2001, is visible in this photo. All seven buildings of the World Trade Center complex, plus other nearby buildings, were destroyed in the attacks by Arab terrorists.

INTRODUCTION

Your grandparents or great grandparents can tell you exactly what they were doing on December 7, 1941, when Japanese planes attacked the U.S. Navy fleet at Pearl Harbor.

You will probably always remember what you were doing on September 11, 2001, when the United States was attacked again. This time, the targets were the World Trade Center in New York City and the Pentagon in Washington, D.C.

As this book went to press, the cleanup in New York and Washington, D.C., continued. According to the *New York Times*, the official death toll in the attack on New York City was 2,830. Only about 700 bodies had been recovered and identified as of this writing. The remains of many others had been found and were being analyzed. One-hundred-eighty-nine people died in the attack on the Pentagon.

Planners are considering ideas for rebuilding the World Trade Center, which was the target of another bombing eight years earlier. Some want to make the space into a park. Some suggest erecting a memorial to those who lost their lives. A construction manager who worked on building the towers wants to rebuild them even higher, as an act of defiance to the terrorists who destroyed them.

Congress passed legislation proposed by the administration of George W. Bush to make it easier to catch and prosecute terrorists. One of these laws gave the Federal Bureau of Investigation (FBI) and other intelligence agencies more power to tap cell phones and track Web sites people have visited on the Internet. Americans are used to knowing that their telephone conversations are private and that no one reads their e-mails. Many Americans feared that the new laws would take away some of their civil rights.

The United States sent warplanes, aircraft carrier battle groups, and ground troops to the Arabian Sea and Middle East. Air strikes targeted terrorist strongholds in Afghanistan. President Bush assured the world that the United States was fighting terrorists, not the people of Afghanistan. To demonstrate this concern, U.S. planes dropped food shipments into Afghanistan. Hundreds of thousands of Afghans, fearing the war, fled to neighboring Pakistan. Pakistan, unable to deal with all the refugees, closed its borders.

Protestors urged peace, saying that bombing Afghanistan is not the way to rid the world of terrorism. They asked Americans to consider why so many people hate the United States. Some people reacted to the attacks by intimidating and hurting Muslims and people of Middle Eastern descent. Others used the tragedy to learn more about their neighbors and to fight hatred and discrimination.

Workers with the CARE organization distribute food to hungry Afghans. The United States bombed Afghanistan in an attempt to rid it of the Taliban and flush out Osama bin Laden, the prime suspect in the September 11, 2001, attacks.

One thing was certain: The terrorists had destroyed lives and buildings, but they hadn't broken the spirit of the United States or Americans' faith in their government.

The words of J. Gilmore Childers, the lead prosecutor during the trials for the first World Trade Center bombing, had become prophetic. Only the date needs to be changed: "For [September 11, 2001] would become a day that would mark for all time the single most destructive act of terrorism ever committed here in the United States. From that point forward, Americans knew that 'this can happen to me, here in the United States.'"

The construction of the World Trade Center began on August 5, 1966, and in December 1970 the first tenant moved in. The twin towers were officially opened for business on April 4, 1973. At the time, they were the world's tallest buildings.

THE WORLD TRADE CENTER TOWERS

Skyscrapers have been a fixture in New York City for over a century. The advent of steel-frame construction and elevators meant structures could rise higher and higher. Tall buildings allowed room for a lot of offices without using up a lot of land. In addition, tall buildings symbolize power.

The World Trade Center was designed to show the world that the United States was an important international trader. The idea was to build something that would be noticed. No one could miss two 110-story towers that dwarfed the city's other skyscrapers. They would be the tallest structures in the world at that time.

When the World Trade Center towers opened, 50,000 people worked there in businesses such as commodities trading, bond trading, U.S. treasury sales, offices of foreign governments, broadcasting companies, the U.S. Secret Service, the federal Alcohol, Tobacco and Firearms (ATF) division, and city and state offices.

The World Trade Center wasn't all business. The Windows on the World restaurant on the 107th floor of the north tower gave diners a spectacular view of New York City and the surrounding areas. Elevators whisked visitors up to the observation deck on the south tower a quarter of a mile above the street in less than a minute. From there a person could see as far as fifty-five miles on a clear day. The shopping concourse underneath the World Trade Center was the largest indoor shopping mall in Manhattan.

The towers attracted more than businesses and visitors—they inspired daredevils, too. In 1972, a skydiver landed on the south tower. In 1974, Philippe Petite fired a crossbow carrying a wire from the north tower to the south tower. With the help of some steelworkers, he attached a cable and walked back and forth between the towers for an hour. In 1977, George Willig used climbing equipment to scale the south tower.

Many people didn't like the way the World Trade Center towers looked. They thought they were boring, that the towers stuck out and didn't enhance the surrounding area. Still, the towers came to define New York City's skyline.

WORLD TRADE CENTER TOWERS STATISTICS

- 7 years to build at a cost of $750 million
- 1.2 million cubic yards of dirt moved
- 110 stories high
- South tower 1,350 feet high
- North tower, with antenna, 1,710 feet high
- 200,000 tons of steel
- 425,000 cubic yards of concrete
- 43,600 windows
- 10 million square feet of office space
- Each floor about one acre in size, as big as a football field
- 50,000 workers every day
- 26,000 visitors to the observation deck daily
- 2 million gallons of sewage produced daily
- 99 elevators in each tower
- Elevators traveled 1,600 feet per minute
- Had its own zip code: 10048

Americans viewed the twin towers as symbols of the openness of American society. A group of terrorists, however, saw the towers as symbols of things they hated about America.

Roots of Terrorism

One of the terrorists in the first attack on the World Trade Center was Ramzi Yousef. Yousef grew up in a conservative Sunni Muslim home in Kuwait. Muslims practice the religion of Islam. In Arabic, the word Islam means submission, or the readiness of a person to follow orders from God.

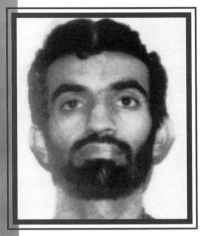

Ramzi Yousef was sentenced to life in prison for the February 1993 bombing of the World Trade Center.

Islam, like Christianity and Judaism, is a monotheistic religion whose followers believe in only one god. There are about 1.6 billion Muslims in the world (there are 2 billion Christians and about 14 million Jews). Muslims are divided into two main sects. About 90 percent are Sunni Muslims and 10 percent are Shiite Muslims.

Ramzi Yousef's father was part of a group of extremist Sunnis who thought all Shiites should be killed. As Ramzi Yousef grew up, these views were impressed upon him. In 1986, Yousef moved to Great Britain. There he became friends with members of the Muslim Brotherhood, an extremist group that supported terrorism.

Meanwhile, a war against the Soviet Union had started in Afghanistan. The Afghan government had changed, and the new leaders showed an interest in making an agreement with the United States. At that time, the Soviets were bitter enemies of the United States. The Soviets feared that under such an agreement, the United States would establish a military base in Afghanistan. To protect their holdings, the Soviets sent troops to Afghanistan in 1979.

Many Muslims hated the Soviet Union, considering the nation to be godless. Thousands of young Muslim men

The fundamentalist Muslim Taliban took over most of Afghanistan in 1996 and imposed their harsh brand of Islam on all the people of the nation.

from around the world came to Afghanistan to join the *mujahideen*, or freedom fighters. Over the ten years of the war, more than 25,000 mujahideen from thirty-five countries fought for Afghanistan. The United States, anxious to see the Soviets stopped, supported the mujahideen with $500 million and supplied them with guns, missiles, and training.

Ramzi Yousef joined the mujahideen in 1988. He spent several months in a training camp in Pakistan learning how to make bombs. The camp was financed by a wealthy Saudi Arabian Muslim named Osama bin Laden. Like the United States, bin Laden used his money to train the Afghan mujahideen to fight against the Soviets.

The war proved disastrous for the Soviet Union. Even though it was the stronger nation, its troops weren't accustomed to fighting in a mountainous country against rebellious guerillas. In 1989, after losing 14,000 men, the Soviet Union pulled its troops out of Afghanistan. Once the Soviet threat had vanished, the United States dropped all support for the Muslim rebels. This action turned many mujahideen against the United States. They returned to their homelands and spread their fundamentalist Islamic beliefs and militant ideas.

Yousef had many Palestinian friends, and he came to believe that the troubles of the Middle East were caused by Israel's oppression of the Palestinians. Since the United States is a major supporter of Israel, Yousef turned his hatred toward the United States. He was no longer fighting for his religious or political beliefs, but out of the desire to punish his enemies. He decided that his method of punishment would be to kill huge numbers of American people. He hoped to make these numbers as high as the deaths from the atomic bomb that the United States had dropped on Hiroshima, Japan, in 1945, killing 75,000 people. Yousef's plan was to make one of the World Trade Center towers fall onto the other. Both would crash to the ground, killing over 200,000 people.

The Bombing of the World Trade Center

To carry out his plot, Yousef moved to New York City in September 1992. Together with another man, Mohammed Salameh, he kept explosives in a rented storage locker. For several months the two men carried explosives into their apartment and worked on making a bomb out of urea (fertilizer), nitric acid, and sulfuric acid.

When the bomb was ready, the two men rented a yellow Ford Econoline van. They packed the bomb into this van. To avoid being traced to the crime, the terrorists reported the van missing before the bombing. Salameh called the police and told them that the van had

Mohammed Salameh was a conspirator in the 1993 World Trade Center bombing.

been stolen from a shopping center parking lot. Just after noon on February 26, 1993, Yousef and a friend drove the van into the underground parking garage of the World Trade Center. Yousef lit the fuses and the two men left the smoldering van. At 12:17 PM the fuses burned down to the blasting caps.

The explosion moved at 5,000 miles per hour through the garage. The shock wave from the blast bounced off the base of the north tower. The vertical steel frame didn't move, but the obstacle increased the force of the explosion. The wave roared through the parking garage, destroying everything in its path. The explosion rose several stories before it finally vented out of an entrance ramp in the garage.

The bomb ripped a hole in the wall of a subway station, sending concrete and metal flying. Cinder blocks turned into dust. A steel fire door blew off its hinges and smashed into a wall thirty-five feet away. Three levels of steel-reinforced

Workers clear debris in an underground corridor of the World Trade Center after terrorists detonated explosives in the basement on February 26, 1993.

concrete floors were blasted away, leaving a hole 150 feet in diameter in the basement. Some 200,000 cubic feet of water and sewage poured in, creating a lake a foot and a half deep across the basement's lowest level.

The first rescue units arrived within minutes. By 11:25 PM, people were taken out of the last elevator after being trapped inside the building for almost twelve hours. At 2:25 AM on Saturday, February 27, the incident was declared under control. Six people had died and over 1,000 were injured.

The FBI Investigation

The investigators found a piece of the rented van with the vehicle identification number on it. They traced the van back to the rental company. Salameh, who had rented the van, wanted to get his deposit back so he could buy an airplane ticket out of the country. When Salameh returned to the rental car company to get his money, he talked with an FBI agent posing as a loss prevention employee there. As Salameh left the rental office, FBI agents arrested him.

After searching Salameh's apartment, the FBI found enough evidence to arrest other conspirators. Four of these men were sentenced to 240 years in prison, the number of years the judge thought the six people who died would have lived. Yousef and the man who drove the van had left the United States the night of the bombing. For two years FBI agents tracked Yousef around the world as he took part in other terrorist activities. In 1995, Yousef was arrested in Pakistan. Six months later the driver of the van was arrested in Jordan. Both men were brought back to the United States for trial. The juries found them guilty. Like the other conspir-ators, they were each sentenced to 240 years in prison. Yousef is now in a maximum-security prison, where he lives in a small cell in solitary confinement.

As the plane bringing Yousef back to the United States flew over New York City, Bill Gavin, the head of the FBI in New York, showed him the World Trade Center towers. "Look down there," he said. "They're still standing."

Yousef replied, "They wouldn't be if I had had enough money and explosives."

Flames and debris explode from the south tower *(left)* of the World Trade Center as United Airlines Flight 175 slams into it. Smoke billows from the north tower *(right)*, which was hit by American Airlines Flight 11 just minutes earlier.

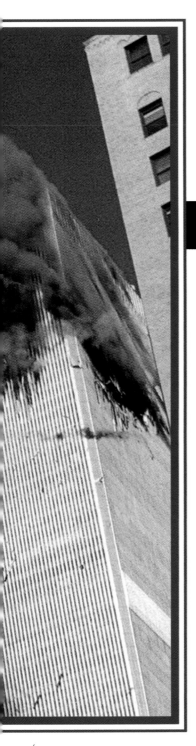

SEPTEMBER 11, 2001

Tuesday, September 11, 2001, seemed to be a day like any other. Airports across the United States conducted business as usual. In Boston, ninety-two people boarded American Airlines Flight 11 to Los Angeles. The plane departed at 7:45 AM. Nearly fifteen minutes later, United Airlines Flight 175 also left Boston for Los Angeles with sixty-five people on board. Shortly after takeoff, men with box cutters hijacked the planes. They took over the cockpits and turned the planes toward New York City.

New Yorkers were enjoying a beautiful late-summer morning in the city. In lower Manhattan, many startled people looked up as

This series of photos shows hijacked United Airlines Flight 175 as it approaches and then slams into the south tower of the World Trade Center while the north tower burns. The impact caused a mushroom cloud of flames and smoke, and rained a deadly hail of debris upon lower Manhattan.

the sound of a low-flying jet caught their attention. Planes weren't authorized to come so close to the towers. Horrified onlookers screamed as American Airlines Flight 11 flew right into the north tower. The time was 8:45 AM.

Black smoke poured out of the gaping hole in the side of the north tower at about the ninety-fifth floor. Rescue workers raced to the scene. Inside the tower, people headed for the stairs. Survivors reported that the evacuation went very smoothly. People helped one another down the long flights of stairs. Many made it to the ground from the upper floors in just twenty minutes. Firefighters and police officers went in the opposite direction, up the stairs, to help with the evacuation. On the streets, crowds poured out of office buildings to stare at the tower on fire.

When workers in the south tower heard the crash, many of them started for the stairs. A public-address announcement assured them that the south tower was safe. Only the north tower had been damaged and there was no need to evacuate. Some workers went downstairs anyway; others went back to their offices.

The Terror Continues

For twenty minutes the nation regarded the collision as an accident. But at 9:05 AM, as television cameras broadcast pictures of the burning north tower into homes and offices across the country, they captured the unthinkable live: United Airlines Flight 175 flew directly into the south tower. The plane hit at about the eighty-third floor and exploded into a giant orange fireball. At that point, it became clear that this was no accident, but a planned terrorist attack.

Hijackers commandeered a third plane, American Airlines Flight 77, and crashed it into the Pentagon in Washington, D.C., killing 189 and injuring hundreds.

The horror wasn't over. At 8:10 AM, American Airlines Flight 77, with sixty-four people aboard, left Dulles Airport in Virginia, headed for Los Angeles. At 9:39 AM, the plane crashed into the Pentagon in Washington, D.C. Twenty-three thousand people work in the five-sided government building, including the secretary of defense. Flames and smoke rose from the western side of the building; part of it soon collapsed.

Fighter jets took to the skies, searching for more hijacked planes. The Federal Aviation Administration (FAA) ordered all planes in U.S. air space to land immediately.

Fearing that other government buildings were targeted, officials evacuated the White House, the Supreme Court, the Treasury, the State Department, and the Capitol. Across the

Passengers on United Airlines Flight 93 are thought to have overcome their hijackers, foiling their plans. The plane crashed in a field in Pennsylvania.

country, potential targets were closed, including the United Nations, the Sears Tower in Chicago, the Space Needle in Seattle, and even Disney World. Most malls, movie theaters, and other places that attract crowds were closed.

In New York City, rescue workers ran into the south tower. They didn't have much time. At 10:05 AM, less than an hour after it had been hit, the south tower collapsed. Thousands of employees and rescue workers never made it out of the building. People on the street heard the deafening whoosh and ran away from the scene. Smoke and grit made it almost impossible to breathe or see. Those who made it out of the danger zone were covered from head to toe in ash and dirt.

At 8:42 AM, United Airlines Flight 93 left Newark Airport headed for San Francisco. At 9:58 AM, an emergency dispatcher received a call that the plane was being hijacked. At 10:03 AM, the plane crashed in rural Pennsylvania, eighty-five miles from Camp David, the presidential retreat. While people tried to make sense of this fourth crash, the north tower of the World Trade Center collapsed. The structure had handled the impact of an airplane hitting it, but the steel skeleton could not withstand the intense heat of burning jet fuel. The columns melted and the building collapsed under its own weight.

When they hit the towers, the airplanes, together filled with about 20,000 gallons of jet fuel for their cross-country flights, released 1.2 kilotons of energy, about one-tenth of the energy in the atomic bomb that was dropped on Hiroshima, Japan. The temperatures in the towers probably reached 4,000° F. The steel simply wasn't able to handle the extreme heat.

On the streets of Manhattan, sirens blared as people ran for their lives. Dust, ash, and falling debris filled the air. Office papers floated across the East River.

Less than two hours after the first plane hit the north tower, all that remained of the twin towers was a nine-story pile of rubble. In the afternoon, another, smaller World Trade Center building collapsed. The Marriott Hotel at the World Trade Center burned down. At least ten other buildings in the area sustained enough damage to make them unsafe.

The nation was stunned. Nothing of this magnitude had ever happened on United States soil.

New York City's buses and subways were shut down after the attacks, so many people were forced to walk home from work and school. *Top:* Traumatized people troop across the Brooklyn Bridge, shielding their faces from the smoke and dust spewing from the World Trade Center as the towers collapse. *Middle:* Office workers caught near the collapsing buildings are covered with dust and ash. *Right:* Thousands of people crowd the roadways around lower Manhattan as they flee the city in fear.

New York City's mayor, Rudolph Giuliani, closed the bridges and tunnels coming into the city. Only emergency vehicles could enter Manhattan. Subway service stopped. City buses carried firefighters and police officers to the scene. Thousands walked across the bridges to Brooklyn or took ferries to New Jersey to escape the smoke and dust.

A controversial figure during most of his two terms, New York City mayor Rudolph Giuliani emerged as a calm and compassionate leader after the attacks. He won praise worldwide not only for leading New York City, but also for helping the entire nation cope with the devastation and fear unleashed on September 11, 2001.

Sorting Things Out

Gradually, the pieces started coming together. The planes that hit the World Trade Center, the plane that hit the Pentagon, and the plane that crashed in Pennsylvania had all been hijacked. Using boxcutters, the hijackers had taken control of the three planes that hit their targets. The passengers on the plane in Pennsylvania, having learned of the earlier crashes through cell phone conversations, were probably able to overpower the hijackers. Although the plane crashed, it didn't hit its target, which might have been Camp David or the U.S. Capitol in Washington, D.C.

TIMELINE OF THE ATTACKS

Sources: FBI and CNN
(All times are Eastern Daylight Time)

7:45 AM	American Airlines Flight 11 takes off from Boston to Los Angeles
7:58 AM	United Airlines Flight 175 takes off from Boston to Los Angeles
8:10 AM	American Airlines Flight 77 takes off from Dulles Airport in Washington, D.C., to Los Angeles
8:42 AM	United Airlines Flight 93 takes off from Newark Airport in New Jersey to San Francisco
8:45 AM	American Airlines Flight 11 hits the north tower of the World Trade Center
9:05 AM	United Airlines Flight 175 hits the south tower of the World Trade Center
9:39 AM	American Airlines Flight 77 hits the Pentagon
9:40 AM	Federal Aviation Administration halts all U.S. flights
9:57 AM	President Bush leaves Florida
10:03 AM	United Airlines Flight 93 crashes in Pennsylvania
10:05 AM	South tower collapses
10:28 AM	North tower collapses

Aviation experts were convinced that the planes that hit the World Trade Center were not being flown by their pilots when they crashed. A commercial pilot would have been trained to fly the plane into a body of water instead of slamming it into a building. Experts also said that the hijackers had some knowledge of how to fly planes. Though the hijackers didn't need to know how to take off or land, they knew how to turn and how to keep flying at a certain altitude.

Heartbreaking images of people missing after the attacks on the World Trade Center were posted throughout New York City for many days after September 11, 2001, as thousands tried to locate their friends and loved ones.

Night came, and with it an eerie calmness. Rescue workers continued to sift through the debris in New York City and Washington, D.C. Hope that anyone would be found alive faded as the hours wore on. Many workers found only parts of bodies. All the remains were put into body bags. In New York City, refrigerated trucks took the bags to the medical examiner's office, where forensics experts set about the difficult task of identifying the remains.

Families of the victims carried photographs and fliers from hospital to hospital trying to find their loved ones. They filled out long forms with details about the missing, such as dental records, scars, tattoos, and jewelry.

Two weeks after the attacks, the number of the missing in New York was about 5,000, including those on the planes and the firefighters and police officers who had gone into the building. At the Pentagon, both on the plane and in the building, 189 people had died.

In Washington, D.C., FBI investigators examined the debris at the Pentagon. The rubble was then trucked to a parking lot, where crime scene technicians sorted through it. This process took a month. Since the Pentagon was considered to be a crime scene, officials did not make public everything they found.

For the first two weeks after September 11, the mission in New York City was classified as a rescue operation, and debris was moved carefully in case anyone could be found alive. When hope of finding any survivors was abandoned, the operation changed to cleanup. Large cranes came in to lift the debris in huge scoops. Barges took the rubble to a 3,000-acre landfill on nearby Staten Island. There, the FBI searched for evidence and parts of the airplanes. Eventually the debris would fill 100,000 dump trucks.

Mayor Giuliani estimated that the cleanup would take a year and cost $7 billion. In a televised press conference, he told New Yorkers, "The number of casualties will be more than any of us can bear, ultimately."

President George W. Bush addresses the nation from the Oval Office after returning to the White House on the night of September 11, 2001.

THE OFFICIAL RESPONSE

CHAPTER 3

President Bush received the news of the attack on the World Trade Center while he was reading to students at a school in Florida. Shortly before 10:00 AM he was aboard Air Force One, the official presidential plane. In case the president was a target, F-15 and F-16 fighter jets escorted the plane on a winding route from Florida to Louisiana. Some hours later the president was whisked to Nebraska. At about 7:00 PM he returned to Washington, where he hid in a bunker under the White House that had been built to withstand a nuclear attack.

After the disputed presidential election of 2000, and after less than a year in office, the Bush administration had to face the terror attacks and a war in Afghanistan. Bush's top advisers at the time included Secretary of Defense Donald H. Rumsfeld *(top)*, Secretary of State Colin Powell *(middle)*, and Attorney General John Ashcroft *(bottom)*.

Federal officials moved quickly to safeguard the nation. Donald Rumsfeld, the secretary of defense, was in the Pentagon when it was hit. He visited the scene of destruction before going to the National Military Command Center on the lower floors of the Pentagon. The Secret Service stationed armed agents on the roof of the White House.

For the first time in its history, the FAA closed all of the airports in the United States. All commercial and private planes in the air had to land at the nearest airports and were grounded for two days after the attacks. President Bush authorized the military to shoot down any commercial planes that violated the airspace above Washington, D.C.

Dale Watson, the FBI counterterrorist chief, activated the Strategic Information Operations Center (SIOC). Located on the fifth floor of the J. Edgar Hoover Building in Washington, D.C., the room has a secure communications system. FBI agents searched through intelligence reports to see if they had missed any clues that would have warned them of the attacks. They looked for coded telephone messages, such as "There is a wedding tomorrow," or "You should come home." Nothing stood out. Over 7,000 FBI agents worked on the investigation.

Throughout the day, federal officials held news conferences to keep the American public and the world informed. On the evening of September 11, the president spoke to the nation. In the speech he said, "I've directed the full resources for our intelligence and law enforcement communities to find those responsible and bring them to justice. We will make no distinction between the terrorists who committed these acts and those who harbor them." He ended the speech by saying, "None of us will ever forget this day, yet we go forward to defend freedom and all that is good and just in our world."

For the next two days, the only planes allowed in the air were military jets patrolling the skies over major metropolitan areas. People found the quiet to be both refreshing and frightening. The airports were closed not only to prevent more hijackings, but also to prevent any terrorists from leaving the country (as two of them had done following the 1993 World Trade Center bombing). The FAA's caution proved to be well-founded when searches of some of the

A member of the National Guard watches as a clerk checks airline passengers' tickets at a security checkpoint at Chicago's O'Hare Airport in October 2001. The terror attacks of September 11 forced airports and airlines to increase security measures.

grounded airplanes turned up box cutters and knives similar to those used in the hijackings.

Heading Off More Terrorism

Two days later, the nation's airports reopened under very strict controls. The new rules included no curbside check-ins, random searches of vehicles entering parking garages, no vehicles parked within seventy-five feet of terminals, no plastic knives at food outlets in airports, extensive searches of luggage, no nail clippers in carry-on bags, and only ticketed passengers allowed on the concourses. The result, of course, was long lines. Most of the passengers gladly put up with the waits for the increase in security.

A week later, the FBI found a manual about crop dusting in a terrorist hideout. The investigators thought that the terrorists planned to use crop-dusting planes to spread deadly germs. Just to be safe, the FAA banned crop-dusting flights and ordered background checks on those pilots and crews.

State officials called out National Guard troops to help with the cleanup. By the end of the week, Congress, acting very quickly, approved $40 billion to fight terrorism and to aid in the recovery effort. A few days later Congress approved an appropriation of $20 billion to help the airline companies.

Secretary of State Colin Powell began putting together an international coalition that would fight terrorism, as terrorist groups exist in more than sixty countries. Powell received a lot of support for the coalition, even from countries that had not been friends of the United States in the past, such as Pakistan and Iran. The members of the North Atlantic Treaty Organization (NATO) declared that an attack on one member was an attack on all the members. The United Nations Security Council unanimously approved a U.S. resolution demanding that all countries crack down on terrorism.

President Bush created a cabinet-level Office of Homeland Security. This office was established to coordinate the forty different agencies that deal with security on U.S. soil. These agencies include the Border Patrol, Customs Service, the Coast Guard, and the Federal Emergency Management Agency.

The FBI investigation into the attacks soon had a name: Penttbom—Pentagon Two Towers Bombing.

THE HIJACKERS

FLIGHT 11
Abdulaziz Alomari
Wail Alshehri, 28
Waleed Alshehri
Satam Al-Suqami
Mohamed Atta, 33,
probably the pilot

FLIGHT 77
Nawaf Alhazmi, 25
Salem Alhazmi, 30
Khalid Al-Midhar, 26
Hani Hanjour, 29
Majed Moqed, 24

FLIGHT 175
Ahmad Alghamdi
Hamza Alghamdi
Mohald Alshehri
Al Qadi Banihammad
Marwan Al-Shehhi, 23,
probably the pilot

FLIGHT 93
Saeed Alghamdi, 20,
Ahmed Alhaznawi
Ahmed Alnami
Ziad Jarrah, 26,
probably the pilot

The FBI discovered many connections among the hijackers of the four planes.

Mohamed Atta was born in the United Arab Emirates. He was a student at the Hamburg Technical University in Germany. He and his cousin Marwan al-Shehhi joined a group in Hamburg that wanted to attack symbolic buildings in the United States. Both men went to a Florida flight school, where they paid $1,500 for training time in a flight simulator. Between September 5 and 11, 2001, Atta drove a rental car into Boston's Logan Airport five times.

Ziad Jarrah, a Lebanese, was also a part of the Hamburg group. He had earned a pilot's license in Germany, but took more aviation classes in Florida. After the attacks, agents found his suitcase in his girlfriend's apartment. The suitcase contained airplane-related documents.

Nawaf Alhazmi and his brother Salem roomed together. They bought first-class, one-way tickets to Los Angeles for $2,400 apiece. Nawaf was on the FBI terrorist-alert list for his connections to Osama bin Laden. Khalid Al-Midhar was also on the FBI terrorist-alert list for his connections with the organizers of the attack on navy destroyer the USS *Cole*,

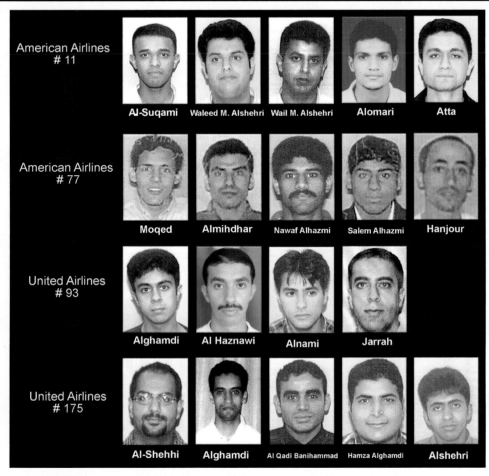

American Airlines # 11: Al-Suqami, Waleed M. Alshehri, Wail M. Alshehri, Alomari, Atta

American Airlines # 77: Moqed, Almihdhar, Nawaf Alhazmi, Salem Alhazmi, Hanjour

United Airlines # 93: Alghamdi, Al Haznawi, Alnami, Jarrah

United Airlines # 175: Al-Shehhi, Alghamdi, Al Qadi Banihammad, Hamza Alghamdi, Alshehri

which was bombed by terrorists in Yemen on October 12, 2000. He was in the United States on a one-year visa.

Hamza Alghamdi, Saeed Alghamdi, and Ahmed Alnami shared an apartment in Florida.

Abdulaziz Alomari said he was a commercial pilot, and was probably traveling with a false ID.

Wail Alshehri and Satam Al-Suqami roomed together. Waleed Alshehri had a pilot's license and a degree from a United States aeronautical university.

Although Hani Hanjour had an expired pilot's license, he had trouble passing his solo flight test at an airport in Maryland.

Mohamed Atta   **Abdulaziz Alomari**

2001 Blue Nissan Altima
Massachusetts Registration 3335VI

Mohamed Atta is thought to have coordinated all four of the hijackings. Investigators believe that he and fellow hijacker Abdulaziz Alomari were at the controls of American Airlines Flight 11 as it plowed into the north tower of the World Trade Center. The car they left at Logan Airport is also pictured. Fifteen of the nineteen hijackers were from Saudi Arabia.

Tracking Down the Terrorists

Some of the first information revealed heroic acts by passengers on Flight 93, which crashed in Pennsylvania. Several of the passengers had called family and friends on their cell phones to report that the plane was being hijacked. When the callers learned that the World Trade Center towers and the Pentagon had been hit by hijacked planes, they knew that their plane was on its way to destroying something significant. Air traffic controllers heard scuffling and someone in the cockpit shouting, "Get out of here." Shortly after that, the passengers evidently overpowered the hijackers and caused the plane to crash in a wooded area.

The FBI quickly had an idea of which passengers had hijacked the planes. The nineteen suspects carried Middle Eastern passports. They left a trail of credit card receipts, rental car contracts, and hotel bills. Several of the hijackers had paid for flight training at schools in Florida. FBI agents checked out the training logs of these schools, looking for others who had been enrolled at the same time.

The hijacker who may have been the coordinator, Mohamed Atta, left behind a five-page document that appeared to be final instructions for the attacks. It included Islamic prayers and urged the hijackers to be optimistic and to crave death. They were to pray and recite the Koran on the night before the attacks. The document also included some practical advice: The men were to check their bags, IDs, knives, passports, and papers. They were instructed to make sure no one followed them. According to their Islamic beliefs, after their murderous mission, they would be granted eternal life.

Exiled Saudi dissident Osama bin Laden, seen here in 1998, is thought to have planned, funded, and supplied weapons for terrorist attacks around the world.

OSAMA BIN LADEN

As the FBI continued to investigate where the hijackers had obtained financial and material support, one name kept coming up: Osama bin Laden. Experts in terrorism said he was the only person who could have masterminded the attacks on the World Trade Center and the Pentagon.

Osama bin Laden, a Saudi who had been hiding for five years in Afghanistan, was suspected of having a part in many terrorist acts, including the 1993 bombing of the World Trade Center and the 1998 bombings of the U.S. Embassies in Kenya and Tanzania, in Africa.

Bin Laden was born in Saudi Arabia in 1957. His father, a conservative Muslim, had four wives and fifty-two children. Bin Laden's father, Mohammed Awad bin Laden, owned a construction company and became a favorite of the Saudi ruling family. He built a palace in Jeddah for them, and then won a contract to restore shrines in Mecca and Medina, two of the holiest places of Islam.

When bin Laden was a teenager his father died. He inherited about $80 million and spent several years partying. After a time, bin Laden lost interest in this kind of life. He married and enrolled in King Aziz University in Jeddah, where he studied civil engineering. At the university, he was taught by scholars who believed that western—specifically American—influence was to blame for the problems of the Middle East. Bin Laden became interested in the Muslim Brotherhood, a group that made him feel guilty about his earlier binges and turned him into a strict, hard-line Muslim.

Bin Laden wanted to create a Muslim world on the Arabian Peninsula that would be governed by divine justice and be free of what he thought was the decadent influence of the West. He believed that the United States supported his goal of making all of the area a Muslim state. After the war between the Soviet Union and Afghanistan ended, bin Laden realized that the only reason the United States had helped the mujahideen was to defeat its rival, the Soviet Union. When bin Laden saw that the United States wasn't interested in his *jihad* (holy war), the country became his new enemy.

OSAMA BIN LADEN TIMELINE

1957	Born in Saudi Arabia
1970	Inherits about $80 million when his father dies
1979	Leaves to fight with the Afghan resistance against the Soviets
1988	Forms Al Qaeda ("the Base"), consisting of Afghan rebels and supporters
1989	Returns to Saudi Arabia, opposes its monarchy
1991	Flees Saudi Arabia and goes to Sudan
1992	Possibly connected to bombing of hotel in Yemen
1993	Possibly connected to bombing of World Trade Center
1994	Saudi Arabia revokes his citizenship
1996	Expelled from Sudan, flees to Afghanistan
1996	Threatens a holy war to drive Americans from Persian Gulf area
1998	Orders Muslims to kill Americans
1998	Possibly connected to bombing of U.S. Embassies in Africa
1998	Establishes terrorist training camps in Afghanistan
2000	Possibly connected to the bombing of the USS *Cole*
2001	Suspected of masterminding attacks on World Trade Center and Pentagon

Bin Laden's Terrorist Network

In 1988, bin Laden set up a terrorist organization called Al Qaeda, which means "the Base." The immediate aim of the group was to establish an Islamic government in Saudi Arabia and to expel U.S. troops from the region. Al Qaeda gave oppressed Muslims money and military training. Members of the Al Qaeda groups signed an agreement called a *beit*.

According to the beit, members would go to a country where a jihad had been declared and wait to be called on to help. While living in those countries, these groups set up "sleeper" units. Members of these units became part of their new communities and didn't attract attention to themselves.

In 1990, during the Persian Gulf War, an angry bin Laden urged the Saudi government to get rid of U.S. troops because he thought their presence desecrated the lands of Islam. Bin Laden said his Afghan Arabs could train the Saudis to protect themselves. He also suggested that his family's construction company dig huge trenches along Saudi Arabia's border with Kuwait to stop invaders. The prince of Saudi Arabia declined bin Laden's offer and instead welcomed American troops.

After this rejection, bin Laden started criticizing the Saudi monarchy. In 1991, Saudi Arabia expelled bin Laden for attempting to smuggle weapons. Bin Laden fled to Sudan, where he continued to speak out against the United States. When the United States sent troops to Somalia in 1992 as part of a United Nations relief mission, bin Laden ordered his followers to attack American interests. In 1994, Saudi Arabia revoked his citizenship.

FBI agents investigating the 1993 bombing of the World Trade Center discovered that several of the men involved in that bombing had fought in the Afghan-Soviet war. They also found records that Ramzi Yousef, the mastermind of the bombing, had phoned Osama bin Laden.

Afghan children play in front of a compound formerly occupied by Osama bin Laden in Jalalabad, Afghanistan, in December 2001. The Taliban gave the exiled bin Laden refuge and provided him with camps to train his terrorists.

In 1996, under pressure from the United States and Saudi Arabia, Sudan expelled bin Laden. Bin Laden fled to Afghanistan, where he found friends among the Taliban, the ruling group of the country. Bin Laden moved from cave to cave in the rugged mountains, guarded by militants armed with machine guns.

The Taliban had gained control of most of Afghanistan by 1996, after a long civil war. Like Ramzi Yousef, members of the Taliban were conservative Sunni Muslims. They passed very strict laws, especially against women. Women had to wear burqas, tentlike coverings that reach from head to foot, except for a small mesh opening around the eyes. Under the Taliban,

The Taliban, a movement of Islamic fundamentalists, emerged from a network of religious schools in Afghanistan and Pakistan during the Afghans' fight against Soviet occupation in the 1980s. Taliban fighters were trained by the American Central Intelligence Agency (CIA), which wanted to use them to defeat the Soviets. Bin Laden also provided the Taliban with financial and moral support. Civil war engulfed Afghanistan in the early 1990s, and the Taliban overwhelmed its rivals and took power in late 1996, imposing a harsh form of Islamic law called *Sharia*.

women could not hold jobs, go to school, be treated by male doctors in hospitals, or go out of the house without a male relative. Men had to attend mosques and grow beards. No music, books, magazines, or any other leisure activities were allowed. To escape this repressive atmosphere, many Afghans fled to Pakistan, where close to two million refugees lived even before the September 11 terrorist attacks on the United States.

The Taliban refused to turn bin Laden over to the United States to be put on trial for the embassy bombings in Africa. After the September 11 attacks on the World Trade Center and the Pentagon, the United States again demanded that bin Laden be turned over. In response, the Taliban claimed that the council of Islamic clerics had asked bin Laden to leave. However, the clerics did not tell him when he had to leave. Later, the Taliban claimed they did not know where bin Laden was hiding.

Under the Taliban, women could not work, go to school, or leave their homes without a male relative. All women were required to wear burqas, which are full body coverings. These harsh, dehumanizing measures left many Afghan women impoverished and deeply depressed.

Although the U.S. government didn't know where bin Laden was, they did know he was a formidable enemy. A spokesperson for the complaints of radical Muslim fundamentalists, he has united many terrorists into one common cause. His leadership qualities, his rich resources, and his strong hatred of the United States have made him a terrifying threat to the world.

An explosion illuminates the night sky over Kabul, Afghanistan, during an attack by U.S. warplanes on October 11, 2001. *Inset top:* Plumes of smoke rise from a Taliban village near Kabul after a U.S.-led bombing run. *Inset bottom:* An F-14 Tomcat fighter plane lands on the flight deck of a U.S. Navy warship.

FIGHTING TERRORISM

CHAPTER

The United States government had decided to fight a war against terrorism, but terrorists are especially difficult enemies to fight. They are loyal to a cause, not a country. They don't want to conquer another country. The terrorists wanted to destroy the American people's faith in the U.S. government. To make matters worse, the United States couldn't negotiate with the terrorists, because there was nothing to negotiate. The terrorists didn't seem to want anything except to destroy the West. The United States refused to use the tactics of the terrorists to retaliate because it is a country that condemns terrorism.

Another difficulty the U.S. government had in fighting this war was that the people involved in the September 11 attacks represented a new kind of terrorist. In the past, suicide terrorists were men in their late teens and early twenties who had been born into poverty, were fundamentalist in their religion, and didn't know much about the outside world. These terrorist groups bragged to the world about their attacks, even taking credit for attacks in which they had no part. Twenty-seven groups claimed credit for the 1993 World Trade Center bombing, for example.

A PORTRAIT OF AFGHANISTAN

Population: 26.8 million
Size: about as big as Texas
Climate: arid to semiarid; very hot summers and very cold winters
Land: rugged mountains
Ethnic groups:
Pashtun 38%
Tajik 25%
Hazara 19%
Uzbek 6%
Other 12%
Religion: Sunni Muslim 84%
Shiite Muslim 15%
Other 1%
Economy: Mostly farming and raising sheep and goats

The new terrorists, the hijackers of the U.S. planes, were generally older, educated, and technically skilled. They knew enough about the United States to live among its citizens without arousing any suspicions. No country or group took credit for the September 11 attacks.

The First Steps

The first thing the Bush administration did to fight the terrorists was to cut off access to their money. The president signed an order freezing the assets of Osama bin Laden and other people and organizations connected to him. This stopped the flow of some of the money, but not all of it.

The military response to the attacks was called Operation Enduring Freedom. The Pentagon sent warplanes and aircraft carrier battle groups to the Arabian Sea. Several thousand reservists were called up to active duty. One problem for the military was that no one really knew who or what it was fighting. When the Japanese attacked Pearl Harbor in World War II, the United States knew who to attack—a country with armed forces. In the fight against terrorism, military leaders had no specific country or group to go after. They would have to use different tactics to fight small groups of terrorists known to be hiding in caves.

In a radio address on September 15, 2001, President Bush told Americans that "This is a conflict without battle-fields or beachheads." He warned the American people that the war against terrorism would be a long campaign.

U.S. troops fighting the Taliban arrive for a meeting with Secretary of Defense Donald Rumsfeld at an airbase in Afghanistan on December 16, 2001.

The first U.S. air strikes were carried out on October 13 and 14, 2001. American and British forces launched precision missile attacks against Taliban military facilities in Afghanistan. This was widely considered to be the first wave of air strikes in what was expected to be a long and sustained campaign to root out terrorism.

During a televised news conference, President Bush told the American people: "On my orders, the United States military has begun strikes against Al Qaeda terrorist training camps and military installations of the Taliban regime in Afghanistan. These carefully targeted actions are designed to disrupt the use of Afghanistan as a terrorist base of operations and to attack the military capability of the Taliban regime."

Many people were concerned that the U.S. air strikes would result in civilian Afghan casualties. And not all of the

Afghan people supported the Taliban. Many of the anti-Taliban forces had formed themselves into a single resistance group called the Northern Alliance. Two days before the attacks on America,

Bin Laden is thought to have hidden in some of Afghanistan's many caves, which he outfitted with sophisticated communications equipment.

the leader of this resistance group, Ahmed Shah Masoud, was assassinated. Terrorist experts believed followers of Osama bin Laden killed Masoud so that he couldn't help in the fight against bin Laden.

By March 2002, at the six-month anniversary of the World Trade Center and Pentagon attacks, intelligence officials worried that U.S. forces in Afghanistan faced increasing danger of being attacked by pockets of Al Qaeda and Taliban fighters hidden in the country's mountains and cities. Experts believed that the United States eventually would be drawn into a long, guerilla-style conflict. The American people were warned that they were still at risk: CIA Director George J. Tenet predicted that Al Qaeda would continue to plan attacks on targets in the United States and at U.S. installations abroad.

Spotlights illuminate the site of the World Trade Center disaster, called Ground Zero by many. Officials estimate that workers will have removed 1.7 million tons of debris from the fallen towers by the time the area is cleaned up.

THE REACTION

In the aftermath of the attacks, Americans looked for someone to blame. Since the hijackers were all Muslims from the Middle East, some people struck out at anyone who looked Middle Eastern or seemed to be Muslim.

Many Muslim mosques across the country received threats that they would be burned, so local police provided them with extra protection. Middle Eastern and Muslim students reported being glared at with hostility. Anti-Arab graffiti defaced buildings. In Tennessee, a Muslim woman was beaten on her way to worship. Businesses owned by Middle Easterners were vandalized and burned. In Arizona, a man was killed because he

Many Americans rallied in support of Arab American and Muslim communities to prevent racist retribution in the days after September 11.

had dark skin and wore a turban. The man was not Muslim, but a Sikh who was from India.

Those of Middle Eastern descent who were natives of the United States resented accusations that they were associated with terrorists. Some quit wearing their headgear so they wouldn't be objects of anger. Legal immigrants didn't want to go to the Immigration and Naturalization Service to get papers or information they needed for fear that they would be questioned or arrested.

One reason for the hatred may be that many Americans don't understand Islam. One of the most difficult ideas for non-Muslims to understand is that of the jihad. The Koran teaches that when Islam or Muslim lands are threatened, Muslims must carry out a jihad of the sword. Mainstream Islam has rules about jihads. Civilians are not to be killed, and terrorism is prohibited. A Muslim should fight only those who fight him. Women, children, and the elderly must be spared. The Koran also says that suicide is against God's word.

Just as different branches of Christianity and Judaism interpret the words of the Bible differently, different branches of

Islam interpret the Koran differently. Although the hijackers may have believed they were carrying out the teachings of the Koran, most Muslims reject the hijackers' version of Islam.

Although the hijackers were Muslims, they were not typical Muslims. They followed an extreme form of the religion. Some experts on Islam speculate that Muslim extremists resent the fact that U.S. culture dominates the world. The extremists think the United States is a secular, or nonreligious, country. They fear that as the influence of the United States spreads, Muslims will lose their language, their religion, and their way of life.

Fundamentalist Muslims such as Osama bin Laden and his followers want to return to a time when society was free of what they consider to be moral decay. They see Israel as an enemy because it pushed the Palestinians out of their homeland. They resent seeing non-Muslims in Muslim territory. They are angry at the United States because it supports Israel. Many groups may feel this way, but they do not resort to terrorism. Fundamentalist Muslims have turned the concept of jihad into an excuse to wage their personal battles.

New York City mayor Rudolph Giuliani urged Americans to judge people by who they are rather than what they look like. In one of his press conferences on September 11, 2001, he said, "Hatred, prejudice, and bigotry are what caused this terrible tragedy, and the people of the city of New York should act differently." His words can be applied to all Americans and all freedom-loving people.

Anti-Terrorism Legislation

In an attempt to prevent future terrorist attacks, Attorney General John Ashcroft proposed the Anti-Terrorism Act of 2001 (ATA). The act would expand surveillance laws to include not just telephones but the Internet and e-mail. The law would also let the FBI monitor the activity of everyone who uses computers in libraries. Since the ATA could possibly take away constitutional rights, many members of Congress wanted to take time to think carefully about the issues.

After discussing the issue for five weeks, Congress gave the administration some permission to expand wiretap laws, but they said that these laws had to be considered again in 2005. The bill, called the USA Patriot Act (USAPA), was signed into law on October 26, 2001.

After September 11, 2001, Americans knew their lives had changed forever. They were fearful after the attacks. They wondered if and when another attack would occur. But while they worried, they went back to work and carried on with their lives. They did not give the terrorists the satisfaction of destroying their society and system of government. While they took steps against more terrorist acts, they were painfully aware that terrorism is a price they pay for a free society.

GLOSSARY

appropriation   Funds set aside by a group such as the government for a specific purpose.

bunker   An underground room, often made of concrete, that is designed for protection during military attacks.

coalition   A temporary alliance to act together on a problem that affects the group.

desecrate   To violate the sacredness of a holy place or object.

forensics   The use of medicine to solve legal questions. Often, this means the analysis of a cause of death.

formidable   Arousing fear, dread, or awe.

intelligence   Information gathered about an enemy.

jihad   Holy war of Muslims against non-Muslims.

monotheistic   Believing that only one god exists.

mujahideen   Muslim freedom fighters.

secular   Things that relate to the world other than religion.

shrine   A place that is considered sacred by a religious group. It is often a place where prayers and rituals are performed.

FOR MORE INFORMATION

American Civil Liberties Union (ACLU)
125 Broad Street, 18th Floor
New York, NY 10004-2400
Web site: http://www.aclu.org

Anti-Defamation League
823 United Nations Plaza
New York, NY 10017
Web site: http://www.adl.org

United States Department of Justice
950 Pennsylvania Avenue NW
Washington DC 20530-0001
(202) 353-1555
Web site: http://www.usdoj.gov

Due to the changing nature of Internet links, the Rosen Publishing Group, Inc., has developed an online list of Web sites related to the subject of this book. This site is updated regularly. Please use this link to access the list:

http://www.rosenlinks.com/tat/awtc/

FOR FURTHER READING

Armstrong, Karen. *Islam: A Short History*. New York: Modern Library, 2000.

Cooley, John K. *Unholy Wars: Afghanistan, America, and International Terrorism*. Sterling, VA: Pluto Press, 2000.

Darton, Eric. *Divided We Stand: A Biography of New York's World Trade Center*. New York: Basic Books, 1999.

Dwyer, Jim, David Kocieniewski, Deidre Murphy, and Peg Tyre. *Two Seconds Under the World*. New York: Crown Publishers, Inc., 1994.

The New Yorker. September 24, 2001.

Rashid, Ahmed. *Taliban: Militant Islam, Oil and Fundamentalism in Central Asia*. Waterville, ME: Thorndike Press, 2002.

Reeve, Simon. *The New Jackals: Ramzi Yousef, Osama Bin Laden and the Future of Terrorism*. Boston, MA: Northeastern University Press, 1999.

BIBLIOGRAPHY

Beyer, Lisa. "The Most Wanted Man in the World."
Time, September 24, 2001.

Constable, Pamela. "Taliban: Bin Laden Told to Leave."
The Washington Post, September 28, 2001.

Darton, Eric. *Divided We Stand: A Biography of
New York's World Trade Center*. New York: Basic
Books, 1999.

Kaplan, David E., and Kevin Whitelaw. "The CEO
of Terror, Inc." *U.S. News & World Report*,
October 1, 2001.

McGeary, Johanna, and David van Biema. "The New
Breed of Terrorism." *Time*, September 24, 2001.

Murphy, Caryle. "Terrorists' Islam not Condoned."
The Washington Post, September 17, 2001.

Reeve, Simon. *The New Jackals: Ramzi Yousef, Osama Bin
Laden and the Future of Terrorism*. Boston: Northeastern
University Press, 1999.

Rempel, William C., and Richard A. Serrano. "U.S. on
Terrorists' Trail." *Los Angeles Times*, September 13, 2001.

Stein, Joel. "Digging Out." *Time*, September 24, 2001

Woodward, Bob. "Hijacker Left Behind Eerie Instructions."
The Washington Post, September 28, 2001.

INDEX

A

Afghanistan
  facts about, 50
  and Osama bin Laden, 41, 42
  and Taliban, 45–47
  U.S. strikes against, 6, 24–43
  war with Soviet Union, 12–14
Al Qaeda, 43–44, 52, 53
Anti-Terrorism Act of 2001, 58
Atta, Mohamed, 36, 39

F

Federal Aviation Administration (FAA),
  22, 32, 33, 35
Federal Bureau of Investigation (FBI)
  increasing powers of, 6, 58
  investigation of the 1993 bombing,
    16–17, 44
  investigation of the September 11,
    2001, attacks, 29, 33, 35, 38–39, 41

H

hijackers, 26, 27, 36–37, 38–39, 51, 55, 57

L

Laden, Osama bin
  relationship with Taliban, 45–47, 53
  role in terrorism, 13, 41, 43–44, 51, 57
  youth, 42

M

Masoud, Ahmed Shah, 53
mujahideen, 13, 14, 42
Muslim Brotherhood, 12, 42
Muslims/Islam
  attacks against, 6, 55–56, 57
  facts about, 11–12

  fundamentalist Islam, 11, 12, 14, 47,
    50, 56–57
  Shiite Muslims, 12
  Sunni Muslims, 11, 12, 45

P

Pakistan, 6, 13, 17, 35, 46
Pentagon
  response to attacks, 51
  September 11, 2001, attack on, 5, 22,
    26, 29, 32, 35, 38, 41,
protests against U.S. strikes, 6

S

Salameh, Mohammed, 14, 15, 17
Soviet Union, war with Afghanistan,
  12–14, 42, 44

T

Taliban, 45–47, 52–53
terrorism
  roots of, 11–14
  U.S. fight against, 6, 7, 33, 34–35,
    49–53, 58

W

World Trade Center
  facts about, 11
  history of, 9–10
  1993 bombing, 11, 14–17
  rebuilding, 5–6
  September 11, 2001, attack on, 19–21,
    23, 24, 26–29
  U. S. response to attack on, 31–35

Y

Yousef, Ramzi, 11–13, 14, 15, 17, 44, 45

About the Author

Carolyn Gard is a former teacher and freelance writer who writes mainly for teenagers. She also does research for members of the Colorado state legislature. She lives in Boulder, Colorado, where she trains German shepherds.

Acknowledgment

The author wishes to thank Norm, who never lost his faith.

Photo Credits

Cover (left) © Richard Drew/AP/Wide World Photos; cover (right) © Carmen Taylor/AP/Wide World Photos; pp. 4, 7, 8–9, 11, 26, 28, 32, 37, 54–55 © Liaison/Getty; pp. 12, 15, 40–41 © AP/Wide World Photos; pp. 13, 46 © Hurriyet/AP/Wide World Photos; p. 16 © Alex Brandon/AP/ Wide World Photos; pp. 18–19 © Chao Soi Cheong/AP/Wide World Photos; p. 20 © Sean Adair/Reuters/Liaison/Getty; p. 22 © Dan Lopez/AP/Wide World Photos; p. 23 © Scott Spangler/AP/Wide World Photos; pp. 25 (top and middle) © Daniel Shanken/AP/Wide World Photos; p. 25 (bottom) © Gulnara Samoilova/AP/Wide World Photos; pp. 30–31 © Larry Downing/Reuters/Liaison/Getty; p. 34 © Reuters NewMedia Inc./Corbis; p. 38 © FBI/Reuters/Liaison/Getty; p. 45 © Geoff Spencer/AP/Wide World Photos; p. 47 © John McConnico/AP/Wide Wrold Photos; pp. 48–49 © Al-Jazeera TV/AP/Wide World Photos; p. 48 (top inset) © Department of Defense/AP/Wide World Photos; p. 48 (bottom inset) © Gustaro Ferrari/AP/Wide World Photos; p. 50 © Dario Lopez-Mills/AP/Wide World Photos; p. 52 © Pablo Martinez Monsirais/AP/Wide World Photos; p. 53 © John Moore/AP/Wide World Photos; p. 56 © Ann Helsenfelt/AP/Wide World Photos.

Series Editor

Christine Poolos

Series Design and Layout

Geri Giordano